WITHDRAWN

Profiles in American History

The Life and Times of

NATHAN HALE

Mitchell Lane
PUBLISHERS

P.O. Box 196 · Hockessin, Delaware 19707

Profiles in American History

Titles in the Series

The Life and Times of

Alexander Hamilton

Benjamin Franklin

Betsy Ross

Eli Whitney

George Rogers Clark

Hernando Cortés

John Adams

John Cabot

John Hancock

John Peter Zenger

Nathan Hale

Patrick Henry

Paul Revere

Samuel Adams

Sir Walter Raleigh

Susan B. Anthony

Thomas Jefferson

William Penn

The Life and Times of

NATHAN
HALE

Kathleen Tracy

Printing   1   2   3   4   5   6   7   8   9

Library of Congress Cataloging-in-Publication Data
Tracy, Kathleen.
    The life and times of Nathan Hale / by Kathleen Tracy.
        p. cm. — (Profiles in American history)
    Includes bibliographical references and index.
    ISBN 1-58415-447-0 (library bound)
    1. Hale, Nathan, 1755–1776—Juvenile literature. 2. Spies—United States—Biography—Juvenile literature. 3. Soldiers—United States—Biography—Juvenile literature. 4. United States—History—Revolution, 1775–1783—Secret Service—Juvenile literature. I. Title. II. Series.
E280.H2T73 2007
973.3'85092—dc22   2006006111

ISBN-10: 1-58415-447-0   ISBN-13: 9781584154471

ABOUT THE AUTHOR: Kathleen Tracy has been a journalist for over twenty years. Her writing has been featured in magazines including *The Toronto Star*'s "Star Week," *A&E Biography* magazine, *KidScreen* and *Variety*. She is also the author of numerous biographies and other nonfiction books, including *Mariano Guadalupe Vallejo, William Hewlett: Pioneer of the Computer Age, The Watergate Scandal, The Life and Times of Cicero, Mariah Carey, Kelly Clarkson,* and *The Plymouth Colony: The Pilgrims Settle in New England* for Mitchell Lane Publishers.

PHOTO CREDITS: Cover, pp. 1, 3—Cindy McGrellis; pp. 6, 9, 14, 17, 40, 41—Library of Congress; pp. 11, 22—Barbara Marvis; p. 33—Hulton Archive/Getty Images; p. 39—North Wind Picture Archives.

PUBLISHER'S NOTE: This story is based on the author's extensive research, which she believes to be accurate. Documentation of such research is contained on page 46.
    The internet sites referenced herein were active as of the publication date. Due to the fleeting nature of some web sites, we cannot guarantee they will all be active when you are reading this book.

Profiles in American History

Contents

*For Your Information

The Continental Army was established in June 1775. The Continental Congress voted unanimously to elect General George Washington as its commander. Although most American colonists at the time disliked the idea of a "national" army, the desire for independence from British rule made an organized military a necessity.

CHAPTER
1

The Battle of Brooklyn

One of the most important battles in the War of Independence would also go down in history as George Washington's worst military defeat. It resulted in the deaths of more colonists than any other single battle in the seven-year conflict. And yet it was the battle that turned the tide in favor of the Americans because of what the British did *not* do.

By all accounts, the more numerous, better-trained redcoats were poised to stop the Revolution in its tracks by destroying the Continental Army just one month after the Declaration of Independence was signed. But thanks to a freak of nature, Britain missed its chance to put a stake through the heart of the Revolution and gave Washington, and the upstart United States, a second chance—an opportunity they would not waste.

What is even more fascinating about the Battle of Brooklyn is that few people are aware it even happened because it is almost completely ignored in American history textbooks.

The stage had been set for the dramatic confrontation in March 1776, when American soldiers defeated the British in Boston. Having secured the important port city, Washington moved most of his troops to New York, another obvious target.

Intent on crushing the colonial uprising once and for all, Britain's King George III sent a massive military response. By August, 430 ships—a fleet three times the size of the Spanish Armada—had been deployed to the waters off New York. They carried 10,000 sailors and additional ground troops. It would be Britain's largest show of military might until the Normandy invasion during World War II 168 years later.

In August, a force of more than 20,000 soldiers streamed into Brooklyn, landing near where the Verrazano Narrows Bridge stands today. For the British, it was the perfect staging post to invade New York because the area was populated by neutral Dutch farmers.

In a 2001 interview with the *New York Times*, history expert Dr. Ray Raymond said the operation "was also the one real chance for the British to win it. New York was the centerpiece of British strategy. The idea was to secure New York, where the British had a great deal of support; cut off New England, which they regarded as the real hotbed of revolutionary activity; link up with a British army coming south from Canada; and bring the whole thing to a halt."[1]

Before dawn on August 27, British troops under the command of General William Howe began their march from Brooklyn to New York. It is estimated that in all, 32,000 British soldiers took part in the battle, compared Washington's 11,000 untrained troops. At three strategic passes, American soldiers were overwhelmed by the sheer number of redcoats, who charged the colonists with muskets flashing and bayonets slashing. It was a slaughter, and the British quickly advanced.

Washington's troubles were just beginning. He was caught off-guard by 15,000 redcoats who had marched all night long to attack his troops from behind his own lines. By noon more than 3,000 Americans had been killed or captured or were missing. The British had lost only 347 men.

By the afternoon of the battle, the Americans were in full retreat, desperately trying to get back to their main fortifications in Brooklyn Heights. The British had blocked many of the colonists' planned escape routes, potentially trapping a large number of soldiers.

The Verrazano Narrows Bridge spans the Hudson River between Staten Island and Brooklyn. It was named after Giovanni da Verrazano, the first European known to sail into New York Harbor (1524). In August 1776, more than 20,000 British soldiers came ashore in Brooklyn, near where the bridge would later be built.

In one of the most stirring examples of selfless heroism, General William Alexander led a regiment of 400 men from Maryland and Delaware in what amounted to a suicide attack on British troops, allowing the rest of the colonial soldiers to flee to safety. The battle was waged near Gowanus Creek in Brooklyn at a site known as the Old Stone House. After six valiant charges, 256 of the 400 Americans were dead; another 100 were wounded or captured. Their sacrifice, however, allowed countless others to survive and reach Brooklyn Heights safely. The bodies of the

Americans were buried a few hundred yards away from the Old Stone House—and today lie beneath an auto body shop.

As his shell-shocked troops struggled to gather themselves, Washington fully expected Howe to immediately storm the Heights—a move that would have effectively wiped out the army and resulted in Washington's capture or death. It would have also ended the war.

The attack never came. That night, a ferocious storm—called a northeaster—blew in and pummeled the area for two days. The rain, wind, and hail forced both sides to take cover and hold their ground. On the night of August 29, heavy fog blanketed the entire region. When Howe and his troops woke the next morning and advanced, they discovered the Americans had slipped away—Washington had successfully executed a silent retreat literally under the noses of the sleeping British troops by having a regiment from Massachusetts row his remaining men across the East River to Manhattan.

Why Howe chose to wait has been argued by historians ever since. Author Robert Middlekauff suggests the general simply didn't appreciate the Americans' passion for independence.

"William Howe was in many respects a solid officer, brave in battle and popular with most of his subordinates. But Howe seems not to have ever grasped the nature of the problems he faced, or if he did he may have been disabled by his sympathy for America. He lacked energy, and he sometimes failed to plan intelligently. He should have struck at Washington's demoralized army immediately after the battle of Brooklyn but chose to begin regular approaches instead. Washington took advantage of his opportunity and, recovering quickly, boated his troops across the river to Manhattan."[2]

That small reprieve allowed Washington enough time to regroup and evade the British troops that continued to pursue his army. Eventually, after defeats at the Battle of Harlem in September and the capture of Fort Washington at the northern tip of Manhattan, the British successfully occupied New York and would keep control of the city until the war ended.

A regiment of 400 colonial soldiers from Maryland and Delaware charged the British near the Old Stone House in Brooklyn. Although 256 men were killed and another hundred were injured or captured, they staved off the British long enough for Washington's troops to retreat safely.

Despite surviving the Battle of Brooklyn, the prospect of a homegrown, untrained army defeating a professional British army remained doubtful until Washington's bold and dramatic decision to cross the Delaware River, which led to a decisive victory at Trenton the day after Christmas in 1776.

"It could have gone either way many times, and when you see how close it was time after time, it's a miracle that it turned out the way it did," observed David McCullough, who authored *1776*, considered by many critics to be one of the most exciting accounts

During the Battle of Harlem, the redcoats advanced as far as what today would be 125th Street but then were pushed back to 106th. The battle boosted the morale of American fighters. It showed they could win in battle against the British. However, the American regiment commanders, Lt. Col. Thomas Knowlton and Major Andrew Leitch, were both killed.

of the Revolution. His book features personal accounts of the participants, bringing the long-ago war very much to life.

"I want people to understand that there have been strong people with a sense of duty and love of country who have served with valor, who were unsung and whose unwillingness to give up has provided us with the freedoms and blessings which we must never take for granted."[3]

Perhaps nobody embodies that sense of duty more than Nathan Hale, a young schoolteacher who is remembered for being the first American spy killed in the line of duty.

King George III

King George III would go down in history as one of Britain's more unpopular monarchs, remembered mostly as the king who "lost America" and for his insanity.

Born in 1738, George III was twenty-two when he succeeded his grandfather, George II, as king in 1760. (His father, Frederick, Prince of Wales, had died in 1751.) A year later George III married a German princess, Charlotte of Mecklenburg-Strelitz. Together they would have fifteen children—nine sons and six daughters.

Although Britain emerged victorious in the decade-long French and Indian War for control over North America, the conflict had been extremely expensive to wage. George's solution was to squeeze the money out of the Americans through a series of unpopular taxes. Colonists were outraged and began revolting. Eventually, his policies backfired and convinced the Americans to go to war to win their independence.

Losing America was the beginning of the end of the British Empire. Inspired by the American success, colonies in other parts of the world began demanding their own independence, creating a series of ongoing military conflicts as George struggled to maintain the empire. The British blamed George for mishandling the Americans and the resulting colonial unrest, and his popularity plummeted.

For any monarch in his or her right mind, ruling at this point would have been difficult. For George, it was devastating. He had been born with the hereditary disease porphyria, caused by abnormalities in hemoglobin, the protein responsible for carrying oxygen in red blood cells. George's case, which was particularly severe, resulted in bouts of increasing mental instability and violence, the first occurring when he was just twenty-seven. Eventually he went insane, blind, and deaf. In 1811, the monarchy was turned over to his son, George IV.

George III spent the last nine years of his life confined to his room at Windsor Castle (left), often in a straightjacket. He died on January 29, 1820.

A popular game in colonial times was hoops. Children would use a stick to roll wooden hoops or hoops from barrels. Although the Hale household was busy, Richard and Elizabeth Hale made sure their children had time to play games.

CHAPTER
2

A Worldly Education

Like most of colonial New England, Connecticut in the mid-eighteenth century was an unspoiled land of meadows, wild orchards, and lush forests. For Richard Hale, the countryside held the promise of prosperity. In the early 1740s, he moved from Massachusetts to Coventry, Connecticut, where he purchased 240 acres of prime land.

He married Elizabeth Strong in 1746. Both were devout Puritans who believed strongly in the value of hard work, the virtue of religion, and the importance of education. With single-minded dedication, Richard built a thriving livestock business, raising sheep, pigs, and cattle that fetched top dollar at markets in New London and Norwich. He also grew crops, built a cider mill, and planted gardens.

By the time their son Nathan was born on June 6, 1755, the Hales were among the most prominent families in the region. Their farm spanned 300 acres, twice the size of an average home-stead. In addition to running the farm, Richard also served as the deacon of his church, was a member of the colonial General Assembly, founded the local library, and served as a justice of the peace.

Nathan was the sixth of twelve children—nine boys and three girls—ten of whom survived to reach adulthood. His childhood appears to have been typical for the times. He was taught to hunt and fish at an early age. Nathan and his siblings were all required to help with household chores, and they also worked the farm when old enough. Sunday mornings and afternoons were always spent in church.

Although strict, the Hales were also loving parents and made sure their children had playtime as well. Nathan enjoyed wrestling and playing ball, and in the muggy summers he would go swimming in a nearby lake. Fun and outgoing, Nathan and his brothers often played good-natured pranks on one another.

Elizabeth died shortly after delivering her twelfth child in nineteen years, leaving Nathan, who was twelve years old, and his siblings motherless. Two years later Richard remarried a wealthy widow, Abigail Cobb Adams, who had seven children of her own. The three youngest moved in, and the already packed house seemed about to burst.

Like all good Puritans, Richard made sure his children were properly educated. After learning basic reading, writing, and math at the local school, Nathan and his older brother by two years, Enoch, began studying under the tutelage of the Reverend Joseph Huntington. They would walk the two miles to the minister's home, where he taught them math and penmanship, as well as Greek and Latin.

An alumnus of Yale College, Huntington was a classics scholar. He instilled in Nathan a deep love of Roman and Greek literature and its tales of larger-than-life heroes who put duty and honor first. Inspired by the reverend's love of learning, Nathan flourished. He advanced so quickly that when he was just fourteen, Nathan was accepted at Yale.

In September 1769, the two brothers set off on horseback for Yale, which was sixty miles away in New Haven and took two full days to reach. Founded in 1701, Yale was the third oldest college in the colonies, after Harvard and William & Mary. The boys roomed together in Connecticut Hall and immediately immersed

One of America's oldest colleges, Yale was founded in 1701. It was named in honor of Elihu Yale, a merchant who donated 417 books, money, and a portrait of King George I to the school. The university encouraged its students to be free thinkers, and they expressed their beliefs openly through debate and organized protests against British rule.

themselves in all the social activities the college had to offer. For two young men raised in the colonial countryside, Yale opened their eyes to a different world.

Outgoing and athletic, Nathan participated in sports, debate, and theater. He also appears to have been a bit high-spirited. His school records show that he was fined for some unspecified infraction, and he also had to pay for a broken window.

During their sophomore year, Nathan and Enoch joined a debating society called Linonia, which discussed the hot-button issues of the day—such as slavery—as well as academic topics.

Almost immediately, Linonia became the center of Nathan's campus social life. Just a few months after joining, he was elected secretary and would eventually rise through the ranks to become the group's president. One of his pet projects was helping establish a Linonian library, donating several of his own books.

Like many American students would be two hundred years later, students at Yale and other colleges in the late eighteenth century were very politically outspoken and regularly staged protests. Most of the time they were rebelling against what was perceived as too much control over their personal lives, such as dress codes, but as agitation grew over British rule, college campuses became a hotbed of political opposition against the Tories.

In broad terms, Tories were people who believed that the right of monarchs to rule was absolute and God-given. Whigs believed government should be at the will of the people. In colonial terms, Tories were loyal to Britain, and Whigs were more sympathetic to the cause of American independence.

In a 1769 letter to a friend in England, the Reverend Andrew Eliot of Harvard wrote:

> The young gentlemen are already taken up with politics. They have catched the spirit of the times. Their declamations and forensic debates breathe the spirit of liberty. This has always been encouraged; but they have sometimes wrought themselves up to such a pitch of enthusiasm that it has been difficult to keep them within due bounds. But their tutors are fearful of giving too great a check to a disposition which may hereafter fill the country with patriots, and choose to leave it to age and experience to correct the ardor.[1]

More than anything, the political involvement instilled in the students the importance and need to be involved citizens. Their academic classes, deeply steeped in the study of classical literature, also stressed the same ideals of honor and citizenship. Despite his busy social life, Nathan remained a dedicated student

Nathan and Enoch roomed in Connecticut Hall. Built in 1752, it is the oldest building on the Yale campus. Other notable residents include Noah Webster and Eli Whitney. In 1965 Connecticut Hall was named a National Historic Landmark.

and avid reader. His letters and diaries reflect an intelligent and thoughtful young man eager to find his place in the world.

As he matured, Nathan became an imposing figure around campus. Aeneas Munson, Jr., whose father was one of Hale's favorite professors, remembered Nathan as being almost larger than life:

His taste for art and talents as an artist were quite remarkable. His personal appearance was as notable. He was almost six feet in height, perfectly proportioned, and in figure and deportment he was the most manly man I have ever met. His chest was broad; his muscles were firm; his face wore a most benign expression; his complexion was roseate; his eyes were light blue and beamed with intelligence; his hair was soft and light brown in color, and his speech was rather low, sweet, and musical. His personal beauty and grace of manner were most charming. Why, all the girls in New Haven fell in love with him. . . . In dress he was always neat; he was quick to lend a helping hand to a being in distress, brute or human; was overflowing with good humor, and was the idol of all his acquaintances."[2]

Like parents today, Richard worried about his sons and the temptations they might be exposed to in college. In one letter he told Nathan, "I hope you will carefully mind your studies that your time be not Lost and that you will mind all the orders of College with care and be sure above all forget not to Learne Christ while you are busy in other studies. . . . Shun all vice especially card playing. . . . Read your Bibles a chapter night and morning. I cannot now send you much money. . . ."[3]

Nathan graduated on September 8, 1773, in the top third of his class. On graduation day he participated in a debate over whether or not daughters should be given the same opportunity to be educated as sons. Hale argued the daughters' cause—and won the debate.

Soon, he would have the chance to put those beliefs to the test.

Colonial Schools

In colonial America, the attitude toward education varied depending on the region. In the southern colonies, only wealthy white males were ensured of getting an education. The middle colonies believed it important—but not important enough to require schooling, leaving it to individual families to teach their children. But for the New England colonies, where most of the residents were Puritans, education was a must—in part for religious reasons. Puritans believed that illiteracy was Satan's way of keeping people from the Bible. Any town with fifty or more families was required to have a school.

Nathan Hale, along with his brothers and sisters, would have first gone to a dame school, which was a little like a day care arrangement. The classes were held in the home of the instructor, who taught both boys and girls to read and write using the Bible and a hornbook. A hornbook was a piece of wood covered with parchment on which the alphabet was written.

After learning the basics, girls would continue their education at home, which primarily entailed learning how to cook, sew, and run a house. Boys went on to "writing schools." Because paper was very expensive at the time, birch bark was often used as writing material. During the winter, these schools were bitterly cold, and the students were required to bring firewood from home. Anyone who forgot—or couldn't spare the wood—had to sit in the seat farthest from the heat.

NEW-ENGLAND PRIMER.

In *Adam's* fall,
We sinned all.

Heaven to find,
The *Bible* mind.

The *Cat* doth play,
And after slay.

The *Dog* will bite
A thief at night.

An *Eagle's* flight
Is out of sight.

The idle *Fool*
Is whipt at school.

Teachers were strict and sometimes cruel. If a student had not properly learned his assignments, he would be forced to sit in the corner wearing a dunce cap. Any student who disobeyed or questioned the teacher would be hit by the teacher with a stick.

Other than the Bible, the boys would study the *New-England Primer* (left), which taught the alphabet by using religious rhymes with a moral. Once they had mastered the primer, some boys went on to other schools or studied under a tutor to prepare for college. Most, however, ended their education and went to work.

The Nathan Hale Schoolhouse was moved from its original location in New London to a site downtown. Hale taught in this building, which was called the Union School, for five months before heading off to war.

CHAPTER 3

Rumblings of Discontent

Once he got out of college, Hale was faced with a familiar dilemma—what do to with all that education. It's probable that his father wished for Nathan to eventually follow Enoch's path and become a minister. Although nobody knows for sure, indications are that Nathan did not have a strong religious calling. What is known is that after his graduation he traveled to New Hampshire to visit his uncle, Major Samuel Hale, a Harvard graduate who was the principal of a prestigious Latin school.

A short time later, with the help of his old tutor Reverend Huntington, he found a teaching job at a public school in the country town of East Haddam Landing. After his lively and exciting college life, moving to a quiet rural town was jarring for the eighteen-year-old. Even though he was well liked by the students and townspeople, he was lonely—and just a little bored.

"Everybody loved him," Hannah Pierson recalled later of Hale. "He was so sprightly, intelligent, and kind and so handsome."[1]

Eventually, as it appears from a poem he wrote, Nathan found romance—or at least a special companion—in East Haddam.

I trust, our Friendship though begun of late,
Hath been no less sincere, than intimate.
Of this I'm sure; I've not as yet regretted,
That to your Company I've been admitted.[2]

Even so, his attachment wasn't enough to keep him in East Haddam. He moved to New London five months later when he was hired for a permanent teaching position at the Union School. His new town, which was a busy port city, was much more to Nathan's liking.

"I am very happily situated here. I love my employment; find many friends among strangers; have time for scientific study, and seem to fill the place assigned me with satisfaction,"[3] Nathan wrote his Yale professor Dr. Munson.

There were around thirty young men in his class, and he taught them math, writing, Latin, and the classics. In 1774, he raised eyebrows among the more conservative locals when he began teaching summer classes for twenty young women from five to seven in the morning. Some locals sarcastically suggested that the popularity of the early morning classes among the town's young ladies probably had more to do with Hale's good looks than a love of learning.

In a letter to Uncle Samuel, Hale said, "The salary allowed me, is 70£ per annum. . . . The people with whom I live are free and generous, many of them gentlemen of sense and merit. They are desirous, that I would continue and settle in the school; and propose a considerable increase in wage: I am much at a loss whether to accept their proposals."[4]

Despite his uncertainty about the position, Hale seemed to have found his calling. He loved teaching and made learning interesting and even fun for his students. Surprisingly, the only complaints he got were from parents who thought he was too nice. Hale believed in giving a lot of verbal support and encouragement to his students—something that was not the norm in colonial times.

His male students were particularly impressed with Hale's athletic ability. Back at Yale, school lore has it that Hale set a broad jump record that went unbeaten for several years after his graduation. At the Union School, Hale—who wasn't all that much older than his students—would entertain them by jumping from one barrel to another and leaping over fences as tall as he was.

The townspeople were equally taken with their nineteen-year-old teacher. One of Hale's good friends, Betsey Adams, later remembered his "remarkably expressive features" and gentle nature. "He was peculiarly free from any shadow of guile. . . . No species of deception had any lurking place in his frank, open, meek, and pious mind."[5]

Sometime during the summer of 1774, Hale became romantically involved with a young widow named Alicia Adams. Hale was obviously smitten—so much so that several of his friends wrote letters warning him against jumping into marriage before he was financially secure.

Yale classmate Ebenezer Williams advised, "A Wife without an Employment is not the most desirable acquisition. I will therefore do more honour to your Judgment than to suppose you entertain designs of marrying at present. But will for once suppose you mean only to endeavour to fix the affections of the young Lady, that you may be in no danger of loosing her. . . ."[6]

Outside his pleasant and increasingly settled life in New London, Hale was aware that tensions between the colonies and Britain were growing. Over the previous decade, Americans had been revolting over taxes, such as the Stamp Act, imposed by the British Parliament and King George. What particularly angered Americans was that they were not permitted to have representatives in Parliament. A Boston minister, Jonathan Mayhew, was an especially outspoken critic and during one of his fiery sermons coined the phrase *No taxation without representation*, which became a rallying cry for colonists.

Feeling it was his civic duty, Hale joined a local militia and, somewhat typically, was elected first sergeant. Even so, like any young man with his life in front of him, Hale's attention was focused on his job, on his girlfriend, on his friends, and on his future.

That all changed abruptly in the spring of 1775. In mid-April, British General Thomas Gage sent troops on a mission to confiscate and destroy guns and ammunition being stored by colonists in Concord, a small town outside of Boston. The soldiers were also ordered to arrest two leading Patriots, Samuel Adams and John Hancock, who were reportedly staying in nearby Lexington.

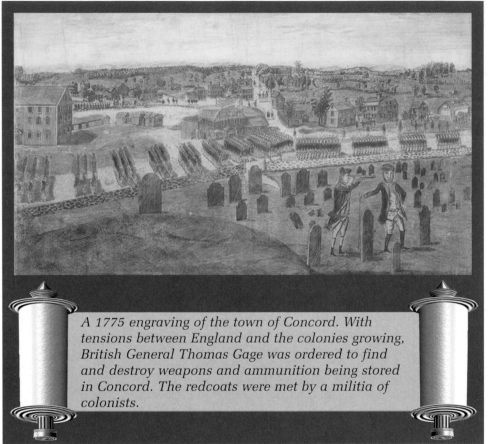

A 1775 engraving of the town of Concord. With tensions between England and the colonies growing, British General Thomas Gage was ordered to find and destroy weapons and ammunition being stored in Concord. The redcoats were met by a militia of colonists.

As the squad prepared to leave Boston, rebels followed them to see what they were up to. Once the mission became clear, Paul Revere alerted rebel militias that the British were indeed coming. A Lexington militia led by John Parker was the first to encounter the British soldiers shortly after dawn on April 19.

According to a sworn affidavit by militiaman Sylvanus Wood, British officer Major John Pitcairn ordered, "Lay down your arms, you damned rebels, or you are all dead men!"[7]

To this day, nobody knows who really fired the "shot heard round the world," but a musket went off and British troops fired on the rebels, killing eight and wounding ten. When the redcoats marched into Concord, they were met by heavy militia resistance and suffered their first casualties, with 73 killed and another 174 wounded. The American Revolution had officially begun.

No Taxation Without Representation

While it's quite probable that the American colonies would have eventually insisted on self-rule, the drive for independence was spurred by colonial anger over taxes—more specifically, over being taxed without anyone representing their interests in Parliament.

Over a ten-year span, Britain imposed a series of levies on colonists that taxed everything from writing paper to tea. The two most unpopular were the Stamp Act and the Townshend Acts.

The Stamp Act, instituted on March 22, 1765, required all colonists to pay tax on every single piece of paper they used, including legal documents, newspapers—even playing cards. The revenue raised from the act was to help defray the costs of maintaining 10,000 British troops to defend the western edge of the frontier, which at that time was at the Appalachian Mountains.

On one hand, the cost per colonist was minimal. But it wasn't the money; it was the principle. It was the first time a tax had been imposed specifically to raise money for the British government. Americans feared that if they accepted this tax, they would be setting a precedent for more costly taxes in the future, so they vehemently protested. Fearing open revolt, Parliament backtracked and repealed the act.

Furious at their impertinence, King George set out to punish the Americans. He used his influence to push through new legislation in 1767 called the Townshend Acts. Not only did these acts impose new taxes on Americans for lead, paints, paper, and tea, they also *lowered* land taxes in Britain.

This time, the colonists were so outraged they openly defied the taxes by buying illegal tea smuggled in from Holland. When the British government passed the Tea Act, which allowed the British East India Company to bypass colonial merchants and undercut their prices, it led to perhaps the most famous outburst of civil disobedience in American history—the Boston Tea Party (above). On December 16, 1773, a group of militant colonists calling themselves the Sons of Liberty dressed up as Mohawk Indians, boarded three British ships and dumped 45 tons of tea into Boston Harbor. When the British responded by closing Boston Harbor, it further fueled the fires of Revolution.

In 1775, General William Howe was named commander in chief of the British army in America. He led the redcoats to a successful occupation of New York and defeated Washington in several battles but was unable to end the Revolution. Howe resigned from his post in 1778 and returned to England.

CHAPTER 4

A Call to Arms

When news of the skirmishes at Lexington and Concord reached New London, a town meeting was immediately organized. Because of his strong debating skills, Hale was asked to speak. With the passion of conviction, Hale told his friends and neighbors the only course of action was for Americans to fight for independence. To prepare the town, he and other local men formed a new militia. Throughout Connecticut, colonists were organizing local armies, preparing for the day when they would have to fight for freedom.

Hale felt it was his responsibility to enlist for active duty, so he wrote the Union School a letter requesting to resign his teaching post before the contract was up.

"Schoolkeeping is a business of which I was always fond, but since my residence in this Town, everything has conspired to render my life more agreeable. I have thought much of never quitting it . . . but at present there seems an opportunity for more extensive public life."[1]

The school granted his request, and he joined the Connecticut regiment. Aeneas Munson recounted Nathan's last visit before leaving: "Hale remarked to my father that he was offered a commission in the service of his country, and exclaimed, '*Dulce et*

decorum est pro patria mori,' "[2] a famous phrase credited to the Roman poet Horace which means: "It is sweet and appropriate to die for one's country."

His first taste of army life was exciting, and Hale displayed the daring that would bring him to the attention of his superiors. The Connecticut troops arrived in New York in late April with few provisions. Up and down the East River were British ships, including a sailboat packed with supplies. Late one night Hale and a few other soldiers rowed out to the sailboat in a small dinghy and quietly overtook the crew in a surprise attack. With the crew locked safely away below deck, Hale steered the ship behind American lines in Manhattan.

The story, and Hale's participation, spread through the ranks of the soldiers, all the way back to New London. Not everyone was thrilled with his display of derring-do. Some friends expressed worry that he was putting himself too much in harm's way and begged him to show more caution.

Even though Hale claimed to have been relieved that he had completed the mission unharmed, the experience had been an adrenaline rush. Despite all he had already accomplished in his life, Hale was still just twenty years old. He was young, he was strong, he was intelligent, and he was confident in his abilities—a combination that friends feared may give him a false sense of invincibility.

In the months after his reputation-making act of piracy, the reality of military life set in. That September, Hale's regiment was stationed in Cambridge, Massachusetts, during Washington's siege of Boston. In July, American troops had surrounded the city in order to force out the British troops trapped inside, who were without access to supplies or reinforcement.

The more he observed, the more troubled he became by the American soldiers' lack of training and discipline. In a diary entry, Hale expressed his dismay: "It is of the utmost importance that an officer should be anxious to know his duty, but of far greater that he should carefully perform what he does know. The present irregular state of the army is owing to a capital neglect in both of these."[3]

Of course, Hale didn't know that George Washington had the same concerns. The commander in chief had been given the task of converting an untrained, nonprofessional civilian army into a formidable fighting force.

During his time at the eight-month siege, which lasted until March 1776, Hale passed the endless days reading. He kept in shape by participating in whatever sports he and his fellow soldiers could organize. He also experienced bouts of boredom and homesickness, missing Alicia. According to family history, Hale came home on leave for Christmas in 1775 and proposed to Adams, who accepted.

Back at the front in Cambridge, Hale struggled with a profound sense of melancholy at the potential loss of life facing both sides as he walked around the Harvard campus, which had been transformed from an energetic place of learning to a military staging area. He found an outlet for his emotions in poetry:

> The muses here did once reside,
> And with the ancient muses vy'd,
> E'en Shaming Greek and Roman pride.
> The Sons of Science here pursu'd
> Those peaceful arts that make men good.
> But now, so changed is the Scene,
> You'd scarce believe these things had been.
> Instead of sons of Science Sons of Mars
> And nothing's heard but sound of Wars.
> Instead of learning what makes good,
> They learn the art of spilling blood.[4]

The siege of Boston finally ended after British troops began deserting in large numbers. General William Howe conceded and withdrew his troops onto ships and retreated north. With Boston secure, Washington gathered his troops and set off for New York, Howe's next logical target.

Even though Washington knew Howe would attack, he needed to find a way to better track the enemy. On August 12, 1776, Washington promoted Thomas Knowlton to lieutenant colonel

and authorized him to handpick an elite group of volunteers from the Massachusetts, Rhode Island, and Connecticut regiments for a special intelligence unit. Dubbed Knowlton's Rangers, these men would be America's first official spies.

The unit was made up of 130 enlisted men and 20 officers arranged into four companies. Hale was immediately promoted to the rank of captain and given command of a company.

Washington's biggest concern was trying to figure out where Howe planned to invade. He decided the best way to gather the information was to send a spy behind enemy lines.

Although today spying is considered a necessary tool governments use to keep an eye on enemies, in the eighteenth century it was deemed distasteful and dishonorable. When Knowlton asked for a volunteer to go behind enemy lines to spy on British troop movement, he was greeted with deafening silence.

Eventually, the youngest captain stepped forward. Nathan Hale broke the silence by announcing he would accept the mission. Hale's close friend, William Hull, immediately tried to talk him out of it, telling Hale he was far too honest to be a good spy—he simply didn't have the character for it.

"I am fully sensible of the consequences of discovery and capture in such a situation," Hale told him. "But for a year I have been attached to the army, and have not rendered any material service, while receiving a compensation, for which I make no return."[5]

Nor was Hale dissuaded by Hull's belief that spying was ignoble. He was more concerned with helping Washington win than with his personal reputation.

He assured Hull, "I wish to be useful, and every kind of service, necessary to the public good, becomes honorable by being necessary."[6]

It was the last conversation Hull would ever have with Hale.

On September 15 or 16, 1776—no one knows for sure the exact date—Hale, dressed as a schoolteacher, slipped into British territory on Long Island. His cover story would be that he was looking for a job. He carried his Yale diploma to further back up his story.

Washington (left) instructs Hale on his mission. The assignment was to sneak behind enemy lines in New York and ascertain where exactly General Howe planned to attack next. Hale was part of Knowlton's Rangers, America's first official spies.

Hale had been gone only three days when Howe launched his attack on New York. Rather than head back to American lines, Hale decided to travel to Manhattan to see whether he could find out anything that would be useful to Washington. For nearly a week, he moved through enemy territory, making sketches of troops and gathering whatever intelligence he could come by. By September 20, he was eager to get out and make his way back to the American lines.

That night after midnight, a fire broke out in lower Manhattan along the wharf. Whipped along by a strong breeze, the fire was

Captain William Hull tried to talk his close friend Hale out of the dangerous spying assignment. He was present when a British officer described Hale's execution to General Washington. Hull included details of Hale's death in a memoir he wrote after the war.

soon an inferno, moving north and west. It engulfed houses along Cortlandt and Dey Streets, which crossed the plot of land where two hundred years later the World Trade Center would be built.

An account of the fire in the *New York Mercury* described the chaos: "Several women and children perished in the fire, their shrieks, joined to the roaring of the flames, the crash of falling houses and the widespread ruin which everywhere appeared, formed a scene of horror grand beyond description, and which was still heightened by the darkness of night."[7]

The British immediately suspected that the fire, which destroyed over a fourth of the settled areas of the city, had been intentionally set as an act of sabotage by the Americans, who would have thought they were going to lose New York anyway. Some modern scholars suggest it is possible that Hale himself set the fire.

Nobody knows for sure. All that is known is that on September 21, Hale was arrested after asking a boatman for a ride up the East River. When he was searched and his drawings of British troops were discovered, Hale knew he would never see American territory again.

Ground Zero

The land on which the World Trade Center towers stood was scorched by the fire that ravaged lower Manhattan in 1776. This plot of land has seen more than its share of history, both high points and low.

In April 1644, an ambitious Dutch farmer named Jan Jansen Damen was given a plot of land near the Hudson River that covered nearly twenty square blocks, making him the first landowner of what would become the World Trade Center site. A prominent leader of Manhattan's Dutch colony, Damen would later be instrumental in the decision that led to the massacre of two nearby Indian settlements.

Like many who came to the New World, Damen dreamed of striking it rich, so he maneuvered to get land grants in the unsettled part of Manhattan north of Wall Street. His plan was to develop the area and become a real estate tycoon. The Dutch governor, Willem Kieft, who was worried about Indian attacks, turned to Damen for advice. While other community leaders, including the governing board's chairman, David Pietersen De Vries, urged the governor to use restraint, believing that as long as the Indians were left alone, they would leave the settlers alone, Damen disagreed. He was particularly concerned because his land was isolated and vulnerable. He pressed the governor to make a preemptive strike.

Governor Kieft agreed. On the night of February 25, 1643, two Algonquin settlements—one on the Lower East Side, the other in what is now Jersey City—were attacked. De Vries' journal recounts the horror suffered by the Indians: "Infants were torn from their mothers' breasts and hacked to pieces . . . others came running to us from the country, having their hands cut off; some lost both arms and legs; some were supporting their entrails with their hands, while others were mangled in other horrid ways too horrid to be conceived."[8] More than 100 natives were slaughtered.

Horrified at the carnage, the governing board expelled Damen, and the governor was recalled by the Dutch government. But the damage couldn't be undone. Not too surprisingly, the other Indian tribes in the area declared war on the Dutch settlers. The war lasted two years and decimated the Dutch community.

Damen died in 1650 or 1651. According to the *New York Times,* "His heirs sold his property to two men: Oloff Stevensen Van Cortlandt, a brewer and one-time soldier in the Dutch West India militia, and Dirck Dey, a farmer and cattle brander. Their names were ultimately assigned to the streets at the trade center site. Damen's was lost to history."[9]

For Your Information

To honor Hale's heroism, Bela Pratt created a sculpture of Nathan Hale for Yale University in 1914. It was installed behind his old dormitory, Connecticut Hall. The above replica of the statue stands in front of the Chicago Tribune Tower. Two other replicas exist: one at his birthplace of Coventry, Connecticut, and one in front of the original headquarters of the Central Intelligence Agency in Washington, D.C.

CHAPTER
5

The Ultimate Patriot

Hale was taken directly to General Howe's headquarters. The drawings left little doubt that Hale was an American spy. Rather than lie, he simply gave his name and rank and the scope of his mission. It has been suggested that he was so forthcoming because he'd hoped to be treated as a soldier prisoner of war, rather than as a spy. His being out of uniform told Howe otherwise, who wasted no time pronouncing a death sentence. What would especially surprise and anger Americans is that the sentence was passed without benefit of a trial. That lack of respect would be remembered by Americans years later when the British denounced Washington's decision to execute a high-ranking British officer, John André, for spying.

Hale was confined overnight in the greenhouse behind Howe's headquarters. The officer in charge of his execution was Provost-Marshal William Cunningham, who would later become notorious for his inhumane treatment of prisoners. While he was in charge of prisons in Philadelphia and New York, more than 2,000 were starved to death; another 250 were hanged without a trial. In what many saw as divine justice, Cunningham would later be hanged after being convicted of forging a check.

His lack of compassion was already apparent in his dealings with Hale, whose final hours were detailed by British Captain

John Montresor. At 11:00 on the morning of September 22, Hale walked to the gallows a mile from headquarters. When there was a delay preparing the gallows, Montresor says he "requested the Provost-Marshal to permit the prisoner to sit in my marquee while he was making the necessary preparations. Captain Hale entered. He asked for writing materials, which I furnished him. He wrote two letters," one to his brother Enoch and the other to his commander, Thomas Knowlton. (Hale had no way of knowing that Knowlton had been killed in the September 15 battle.) Then Hale "asked for a clergyman to attend him. It was refused. He then asked for a Bible; that too was refused by his inhuman jailer."[1]

The makeshift gallows was simply a noose thrown over a tree limb, with a ladder placed beneath it. Hale, his hands still tied behind his back, climbed the ladder.

When Cunningham asked if Hale had any last words, he turned to face the troops who had gathered to watch his execution and paraphrased a line from a play about Cato written by Joseph Addison. However, what he said exactly may never be truly known.

A *Newsday* feature by George DeWan says the story has changed over the years.

> A 1777 newspaper article reported Hale as saying that "if he had ten thousand lives, he would lay them all down, if called to it, in defence of his injured, bleeding country." Four years later another newspaper story quoted Hale's last words as: ". . . my only regret is, that I have not more lives than one to offer in its service." Hull's 1848 memoirs give us the pithier version we know today: "I only regret that I have but one life to lose for my country."[2]

When Hale was finished speaking, the noose was tightened around his neck, and before the ladder could be yanked out from under him, Nathan stepped off.

Later that day, Montresor arrived at the American encampment under a flag of truce to discuss a possible prisoner exchange with Washington. It was only then that Washington learned that Hale had been captured and executed. Montresor also met with

According to British officers present, Hale showed no fear when led to the gallows. Although nobody is exactly sure of his last words, his willingness to die for independence would inspire Americans for over 200 years.

William Hull, who wanted to know the details of Hale's last hours. News of his execution spread quickly through the camp.

While grieving the execution of their friend, being a soldier carries an inherent risk of death. What outraged Hull and the other soldiers the most was that Cunningham left Hale's body swinging from the tree for three days. Enoch only learned his brother had been killed after someone reported seeing his body displayed. Cunningham also taunted the Americans by displaying Hale's diploma and the letters he had written—which he later destroyed.

According to Montresor, "The Provost-Marshal destroyed the letters, and assigned a reason that the rebels should not know

Major André was stopped by Patriots in Tarrytown, New York, on September 23, 1780. In his boot were papers that revealed negotiations between American General Benedict Arnold and the British. André was tried and found guilty of spying.

that they had a man in their army who could die with so much firmness."[3]

Years later, Hull would offer a touching eulogy to the memory of his friend. "There was no young man who gave fairer promise of an enlightened and devoted service to his country, than this my friend and companion in arms. His naturally fine intellect had been carefully cultivated, and his heart was filled with generous emotions; but, like the soaring eagle, the patriotic ardor of his soul 'winged the dart which caused his destruction.' "[4]

Although Hale's death had been widely reported, it wasn't until the furor surrounding the execution of Major André four years later that many Americans began to embrace Hale as a national hero. An editorial in the *London Courant and Westminster Chronicle*

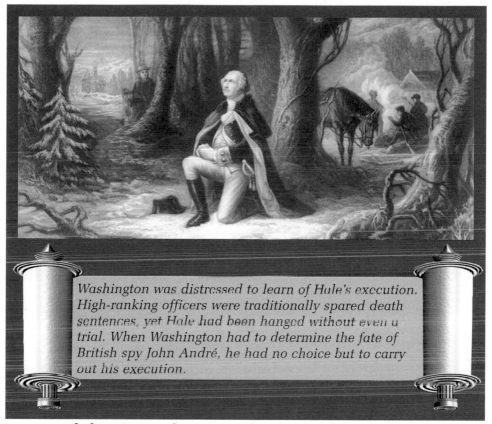

Washington was distressed to learn of Hale's execution. High-ranking officers were traditionally spared death sentences, yet Hale had been hanged without even a trial. When Washington had to determine the fate of British spy John André, he had no choice but to carry out his execution.

expressed the views of many: "The death of the unfortunate and much lamented Major André being industriously represented to the public, as a cruel and unprecedented stretch of power on the part of the Americans, a person who was in the English army, and at that period serving under General Howe, thinks proper to state to the public, and recal [sic] to their minds the story of Major Hale."[5]

From that time on, Nathan Hale came to symbolize honor, patriotism, and courage. The CIA honors him as the first agent killed in the line of duty. Connecticut has named him the official state hero, and there are statues commemorating him in several states. His childhood home is now a historical landmark.

Shakespeare once wrote, "Some are born great, some achieve greatness and some have greatness thrust on them."[6] In Nathan Hale's case, all three seem to apply.

Major André

The British weren't the only ones who took a dim view of spying. In October 1776, the Second Continental Congress decreed that anyone found guilty of spying against the United States would hang. That declaration would put George Washington in the unenviable position of having to condemn a military associate for whom he had great respect and admiration.

Major John André was a highly respected officer when he was put in charge of British Secret Intelligence under General Henry Clinton in 1779. In May of that year, he was contacted by American General Benedict Arnold, who offered to surrender Fort West Point in exchange for money. West Point, which housed the American army, was also a crucial strategic location—if it fell to the British, it would gain them unencumbered access into New England.

In September of 1780, André was sent to negotiate the final details of how Arnold would surrender West Point. A British ship slipped up the Hudson and dropped him off in American-held territory. Before André could make it back, the ship came under American fire and had to go downriver, forcing André to go overland out of American territory. He was actually back in British territory when he was captured by three Americans posing as British soldiers. When they searched André, they discovered the documents from Arnold.

Before Arnold could be arrested for treason, he learned of André's capture and escaped, eventually settling in Canada. André wasn't so fortunate. He was put on trial and found guilty of spying, since he had gone behind enemy lines out of uniform.

The British were incensed that the Americans would break a longstanding, tacit gentleman's agreement that captured generals would be held as prisoners and not executed. Washington offered to exchange André for Benedict Arnold—who most Americans thought deserved death over André. The British declined.

In the end, the decision to hang Nathan Hale without even benefit of a trial—and to leave his body displayed for three days—left Washington little choice but to carry out the sentence. On October 2, 1780, John André was hanged in Tappan, New York.

Chapter Notes

Chapter 1 The Battle of Brooklyn

1. Elliott Rebhun, "Washington Fought Here—Who Knew?: On 225th Anniversary, Battle of Brooklyn Is Little-Known Chapter," *New York Times*, August 25, 2001.

2. Robert Middlekauff, *The Glorious Cause: The American Revolution, 1763–1789* (New York: Oxford University Press, 1985), p. 577.

3. Susan L. Rife, "The Nation's Most Critical Year," *Sarasota Herald Tribune*, June 26, 2005, p. E4.

Chapter 2 A Worldly Education

1. James Axtell, *The School Upon the Hill: Education and Society in Colonial New England* (New Haven: Yale University Press, 1974), p. 242.

2. Benson J. Lossing, *The Two Spies: Nathan Hale and John André* (New York: D. Appleton, 1903), p. 5.

3. The Official Nathan Hale Website (run by Connecticut's Antiquarian & Landmarks Society) http://www.hartnet.org/als/nathanhale/Chronology.htm

Chapter 3 Rumblings of Discontent

1. The Official Nathan Hale Website (run by Connecticut's Antiquarian & Landmarks Society) http://www.hartnet.org/als/nathanhale/Chronology.htm

2. Ibid.

3. George Dudley Seymour, *Documentary Life of Nathan Hale* (privately published, 1941), p. 26.

4. Ibid., p. 26.

5. George Dudley Seymour, *Captain Nathan Hale, Major John Palgrave Wyllys, A Degenerate History*. New Haven, CT: Privately Published, 1933, p. xviii.

6. George Dudley Seymour, *Documentary Life of Nathan Hale*, 1941, p. 26.

7. EyeWitness to History: "Battle at Lexington Green, 1775" (posted 2001), http://64.70.155.140/lexington.htm.

Chapter 4 A Call to Arms

1. George Dudley Seymour, *Documentary Life of Nathan Hale* (privately published, 1941), p. 40.

2. Ibid., p. 380.

3. Robin Kadison Berson, *Young Heroes in World History*. Westport, CT: Greenwood Press. 1999, p. 108.

4. Seymour, p. 93.

5. George DeWan, "Nathan Hale: Failed Spy, Superb Patriot," *Long Island: Our Story*, http://www.newsday.com/community/guide/lihistory/ny-history-hs413a,0,6240190.story

6. Seymour, p. 309.

7. Eric Lipton, "Ground Zero: Before the Fall," *New York Times*, June 27, 2004, n.p. http://www.wirednewyork.com/forum/showthread.php?t=5062

8. Ibid.

9. Ibid.

Chapter 5 The Ultimate Patriot

1. John Bakeless, *Turncoats, Traitors, and Heroes* (Philadelphia: J. B. Lippincott, 1959), p. 120.

2. George DeWan, "Nathan Hale: Failed Spy, Superb Patriot," *Long Island: Our Story*, http://www.newsday.com/community/guide/lihistory/ny-history-hs413a,0,6240190.story

3. Bakeless, p. 120.

4. George Dudley Seymour, *Documentary Life of Nathan Hale* (privately published, 1941), p. 308.

5. Nathan Hale Homestead http://www.hartnet.org/als/nathanhale/educational.htm

6. William Shakespeare, *Shakespeare's Twelfth Night: Or, What You Will*. Contributors: William Allan Neilson, editor. Chicago: Scott Foresman, 1903, p. 154.

Chronology

1746   Parents Richard Hale and Elizabeth Strong marry.

1747   Elizabeth gives birth to first of twelve children, Samuel.

1755   Nathan Hale is born on June 6 in Coventry, Connecticut.

1767   Elizabeth dies at 40, shortly after giving birth to her twelfth child.

1769   Richard marries Abigail Cobb Adams.

1773   Nathan graduates from Yale on September 8; he accepts his first teaching position in East Haddam Landing.

1774   He accepts teaching job at Union School in New London, Connecticut, in March.

1775   Connecticut General Assembly commissions him as first lieutenant in July; he is stationed with army outside Boston starting in September; proposes to Alicia Adams in December.

1776   In March, army relocates to New York; Hale goes on reconnaissance missions. He is invited to join Knowlton's Rangers in early September, then volunteers for top-secret spying mission on September 8. On September 22, he is hanged as a spy.

1799   Hale's famous last words are published in Hannah Adams's *Summary History of New England*.

1914   Bela Pratt creates a sculpture of Hale for Yale University.

1925   Nathan Hale is commemorated on a U.S. postage stamp.

1985   He is named Connecticut's official state hero.

Timeline in History

1704 America's first newspaper is published in Cambridge, Massachusetts.

1719 Daniel Defoe writes *Robinson Crusoe*.

1728 Dutch explorer Vitus Bering discovers strait between westernmost North America and easternmost Asia.

1741 Benjamin Franklin invents the Franklin—or potbellied—stove.

1747 British Navy begins issuing limes to sailors to fight scurvy.

1751 China invades Tibet.

1754 The Seven Years' War begins between France and Britain over control of New England.

1762 Catherine the Great takes Russian throne.

1763 Canada becomes British territory.

1769 Napoléon Bonaparte is born.

1772 Captain James Cook begins second voyage to map South Pacific.

1775 The battle at Concord, Massachusetts, in April begins the Revolutionary War.

1776 The Continental Army defeats the British in Boston (March). The British route the Americans at the Battle of Brooklyn (August) and occupy New York.

1780 British Major John André is hanged as a spy.

1781 British surrender at Yorktown, Virginia, ending the occupation of New York and the war. Articles of Confederation establish first U.S. government.

1786 Shays's Rebellion leads to calls for stronger central government, resulting in replacing the Articles of Confederation with the U.S. Constitution.

1789 Crewmen mutiny on the HMS *Bounty*. The French Revolution begins. George Washington is elected first U.S. president.

1791 Mozart dies.

1793 Eli Whitney invents the cotton gin.

1799 The Rosetta Stone is discovered in Egypt.

1803 Jefferson negotiates Louisiana Purchase, doubling the size of the United States.

Further Reading

For Young Adults

Bakeless, John, and Katherine Bakeless. *Spies of the Revolution*. New York: J.B. Lippincott Company, 1962.

Davis, Burke. *Black Heroes of the American Revolution*. New York: Harcourt Brace Jovanovich, 1976.

Duncan, Lois. *Major André: Brave Enemy*. Illustrated by Tran Mawicke. New York: Putnam, 1969.

Lough, Loree. *Nathan Hale: Revolutionary Hero*. Philadelphia: Chelsea House, 1999.

Krizner, L. J., and Lisa Sita. *Nathan Hale: Patriot and Martyr of the American Revolution*. New York: PowerPlus Books, 2002.

Works Consulted

Axtell, James. *The School Upon the Hill: Education and Society in Colonial New England*. New Haven, Connecticut: Yale University Press, 1974.

Bakeless, John. *Turncoats, Traitors, and Heroes*. Philadelphia: J. B. Lippincott, 1959.

Berson, Robin Kadison. *Young Heroes in World History*. Westport, Connecticut: Greenwood Press, 1999.

DeWan, George. "Nathan Hale: Failed Spy, Superb Patriot." *Long Island: Our Story*, http://www.newsday.com/community/guide/lihistory/ny-history-hs413a,0,6240190.story

Fleming, Thomas. *1776: Year of Illusions*. New York: W. W. Norton, 1975.

Lipton, Eric. "Ground Zero: Before the Fall," *New York Times*, June 27, 2004.

Lossing, Benson J. *The Two Spies: Nathan Hale and John André*. New York: D. Appleton, 1903.

Middlekauff, Robert. *The Glorious Cause: The American Revolution, 1763–1789*. New York: Oxford University Press, 1985.

Rebhun, Elliott. "Washington Fought Here—Who Knew?: On 225th Anniversary, Battle of Brooklyn Is Little-Known Chapter." *New York Times*, August 25, 2001.

Rife, Susan L. "The Nation's Most Critical Year," *Sarasota Herald Tribune*, June 26, 2005, p. E4.

Seymour, George Dudley. *Documentary Life of Nathan Hale*. Privately printed,1941; published Whitefish, Montana: Kessinger Publishing, 2006.

On the Internet

Connecticut Society of the Sons of the American Revolution
http://www.ctssar.org/patriots/nathan_hale_2.htm

EyeWitness to History: "Battle at Lexington Green, 1775,"
http://64.70.155.140/lexington.htm

Nathan Hale Homestead
http://www.hartnet.org/als/nathanhale/educational.htm

The Official Nathan Hale Website (run by Connecticut's Antiquarian & Landmarks Society)
http://www.hartnet.org/als/nathanhale/

Glossary

adrenaline (uh-DREH-nuh-lin)
A chemical the body produces in stressful or exciting situations to help ensure survival.

armada (ar-MAH-duh)
A large fleet of ships.

furor (FYUR-ur)
An uproar or commotion.

hemoglobin (HEE-muh-GLOH-bin)
An iron-containing protein in red blood cells that carries oxygen.

ignoble (ig-NOH-bul)
Not honorable.

marquee (mar-KEE)
A large tent or canopy.

preemptive (pree-EMP-tiv)
Done first or early to prevent or deter a situation from occurring.

provost-marshal (PROH-vohst MAR-shul)
An officer in charge of the military police.

rural (RUH-rul)
Relating to country life.

Index